Turn On To Canada

Chuck Davis

General Editors
Carol Langford
Chuck Heath

Teacher Consultants
Muriel Carriere
Mary James
Shirley Koleszar

Illustrations by Jim Rimmer

Explorations A Canadian Social Studies Program for Elementary Schools

Douglas & McIntyre (Educational) Ltd.
1615 Venables Street
Vancouver, British Columbia V5L 2H1

Canadian Cataloguing in Publication Data

Davis, Chuck, 1935–
  Turn on to Canada

  (Explorations : a Canadian social studies program
for elementary schools. Exploring Canada)
  ISBN 0-88894-864-6

  1. Canada — Problems, exercises, etc.
  2. Canada — Juvenile literature.
  I. Title. II. Series.
  FC61.D38   j971.064'6   C82-091304-9
  F1008.2.D38

Printed and bound in Canada.

Contents

Canada is very big. From one side of our country to the other, the longest distance is 5187 km (kilometres).

Imagine walking right across Canada at your normal speed. If you walk all day and all night and never stop, it will take you 54 days!

It will be an amazing walk. You will see millions of people, all different.

You will also see broad lakes and sparkling rivers. You will see high frosty mountains and low green valleys. There are places where snow hardly ever falls. There are places covered with snow that *never* melts.

4

There are big busy cities and small quiet villages. There are farms and factories. There are long highways swarming with fast cars. There are dusty country roads with hardly anyone on them. You will see that Canada has many different places and people.

Canada is not just big. It's crammed with all kinds of interesting stuff. That's what this book is about.

We can't walk for 54 days to see our country. So we are going to look at Canada in another way.

We are going to open the doors to a special "television studio." You will be a "contestant." Contestants are people who play quiz games on TV. The questions on the special "TV show" are all about Canada. You will find clues to the answers in the drawings and the maps and in other questions.

You are now in the TV studio. The quiz leader is ready to begin. The cameras are coming in on you. The microphones are turning on. 3,2,1 . . .

5

1

Shapes
of Canada

1 Welcome to the *Turn On To Canada* quiz show. Our first program is called "Shapes of Canada." We are going to start by looking at the picture below. What do you think it is?

2 This view of Earth from space is the one astronauts see. In fact, one astronaut said this view of Earth reminded him of a big blue . . . what?

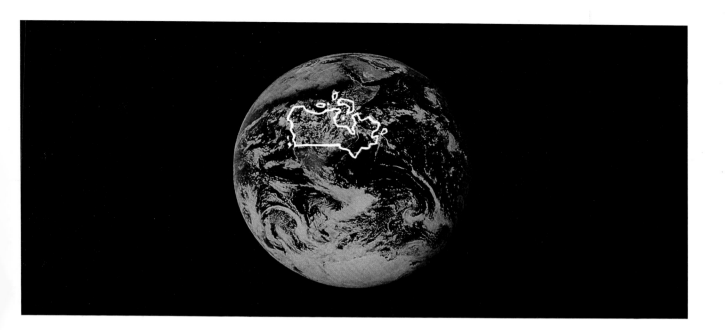

3 Now we have moved closer to the Earth's surface. Below the clouds we can see hugh areas of land. They are called continents. What do you call the *country* that is outlined in the picture?

4 Would we really see *lines* like this, showing where Canada is?

5 The people who live in all the different countries of the world decide what land belongs to their own country. They draw lines on maps to show where their country stops and someone else's country begins. Do you know what those lines between countries are called?

6 Many of us in Canada live very near a border that separates us from another country. What country?

Western red lily
Saskatchewan

YUKON TERRITORY

NORTHWEST TERRITORIES

BRITISH COLUMBIA

ALBERTA

SASKATCHEWAN

MANITOBA

ONTARIO

N
W E
S

7 There are borders *inside* countries, too. Look at this big map. In the southern part of Canada there are 10 different areas. We have made each one a different colour. What are those areas called?

8 Do you live in a province? Which one?

9 Point to your province on this map.

10 How many provinces are there?

11 Now look at the northern part of Canada on the map. The two coloured areas shown there are not provinces. What are they called?

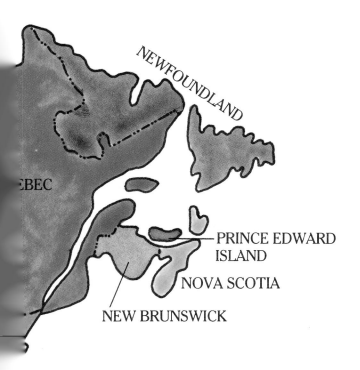

NEWFOUNDLAND

EBEC

— PRINCE EDWARD ISLAND

NOVA SCOTIA

NEW BRUNSWICK

12 Oh, oh, it's time for a Bing Bong—a bonus question!

Look at the drawing. It's a letter W chasing a tank. Mix up the letters shown here. You will find the name of one of the provinces. Which one?

W CHASES A TANK

13 Look again at the big map of Canada. Which province is an island?

14 Which territory is the biggest?

15 Which province is the biggest?

16 Look at the compass rose. What do the letters N, E, S and W stand for?

17
Which province reaches farthest south?

18
Which province reaches farthest north?

19
Farthest east?

20
Farthest west?

21
Can you name all the provinces that touch the Northwest Territories?

Flag of the Northwest Territories

25 Rain falls on the Rocky Mountains and runs down and makes rivers. Can you find a river that starts in the Rockies?

26 Suppose you dropped a ping-pong ball into the Fraser River. It floats away. Where will the ball end up? Follow it on the map!

22 Here is a map of British Columbia. What is the name of the ocean to the west of this province?

23 British Columbia has more of something than any other province. Can you tell from the map what it is?

24 The mountains nearest the ocean are called the Coast Mountains. What do you call the mountains on the east side of British Columbia?

14

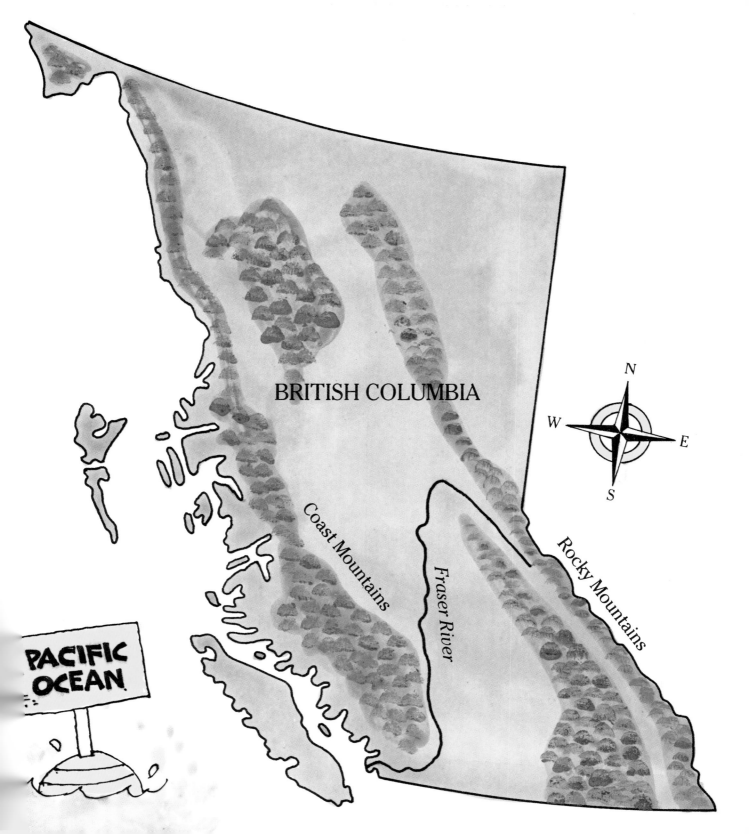

27 See all those dots on the next page? They are People Dots. All the dots together stand for all the people in Canada. There are 24 000 000 (24 million) people living in Canada. There are 2400 People Dots in these jars. That means that inside each little dot are 10 000 people.

Now, which province or territory has the fewest people? Look for the jar with the least number of People Dots.

Which province has the most people? (Remember, look at the jars for your clues.)

28 Which province has more people—British Columbia or Alberta?

True or false: Manitoba has five times as many people as Quebec.

This list will tell you how many dots are in the jar for each province and territory.

	People Dots
Ontario	863
Quebec	644
British Columbia	274
Alberta	224
Manitoba	103
Saskatchewan	96
Nova Scotia	85
New Brunswick	70
Newfoundland	57
Prince Edward Island	12
Northwest Territories	5
Yukon Territory	2

29 How many of the 10 provinces and 2 territories can you name from memory? Don't look at your book.

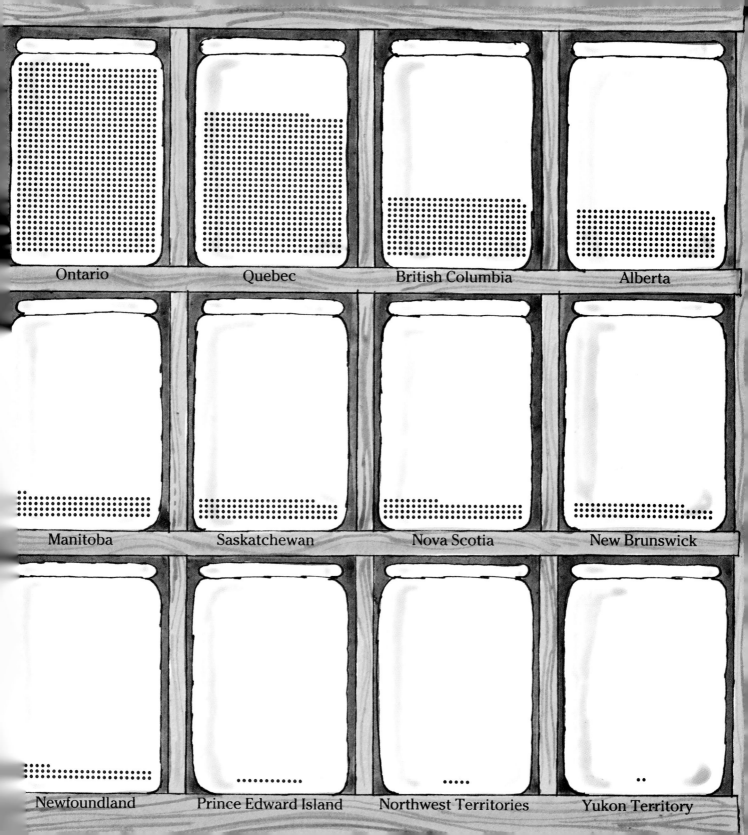

Ontario

Quebec

British Columbia

Alberta

Manitoba

Saskatchewan

Nova Scotia

New Brunswick

Newfoundland

Prince Edward Island

Northwest Territories

Yukon Territory

Trillium
Ontario

30 Look at the maps in this book. Many of them show big areas of water inside Canada. They are not rivers. What are they?

31 Now look below at the five huge lakes. They are just south of Ontario. Because these lakes are so big, they are called the Great Lakes. Can you name them? Can you find all five on the big map on pages 10 and 11?

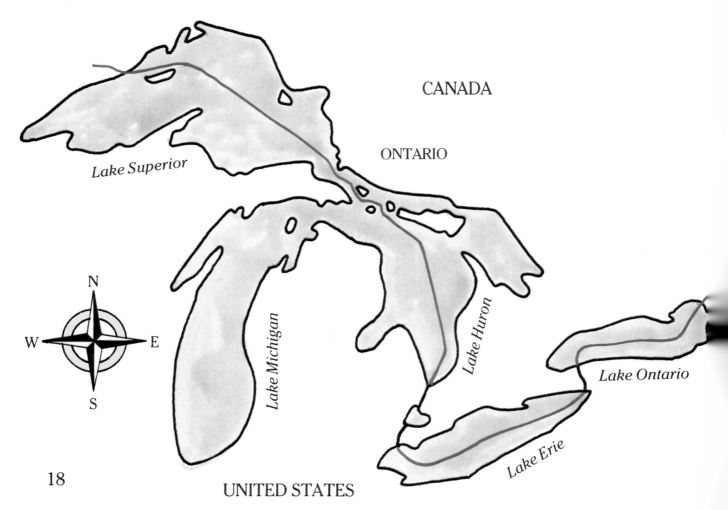

CANADA

ONTARIO

Lake Superior

N
W   E
S

Lake Michigan

Lake Huron

Lake Ontario

Lake Erie

UNITED STATES

32 There is an easy way to remember the names of those five lakes. Just think of the word HOMES. Can you guess why?

33 One of the Great Lakes is not in Canada. What is its name?

34 Are any of the Great Lakes entirely inside Canada?

35 The four Great Lakes that are partly in Canada all touch the same province. Which one?

Flag of Ontario

19

36 Time for another Bing Bong question!

Once upon a time there was a place called BOYITOBA. What was it called when it grew up?

37 Look at the area of water called Hudson Bay. A bay looks like a big bite out of the land. What provinces and territories touch Hudson Bay?

38 The territories are a huge part of Canada. Even so, very few people live in them. That is one reason they are not provinces yet. The Northwest Territories is 600 times bigger than tiny Prince Edward Island. But which one has more people? Look at the people jars on page 17.

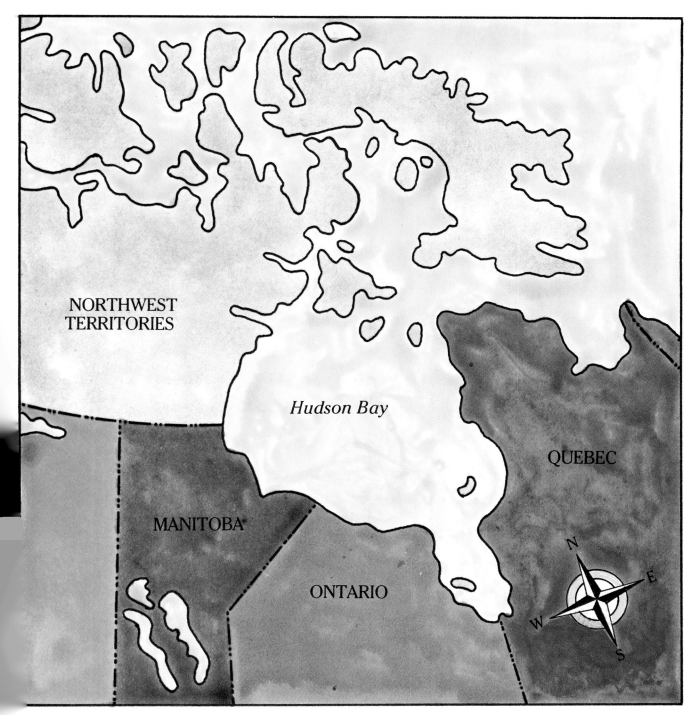

NORTHWEST
TERRITORIES

Hudson Bay

QUEBEC

MANITOBA

ONTARIO

N
E
W
S

39 Look at the drawings on this page. Can you tell each province and territory by its shape alone? Here are some hints:

Prince Edward Island is the smallest province.

Yukon Territory is shaped a bit like a large triangle.

Part of Newfoundland is an island. Another part is on the Canadian mainland. Both parts are shaped a bit like triangles.

Nova Scotia is also in two pieces. It is much smaller than Newfoundland.

One part of Quebec is separated from the largest part by a river.

The top of Alberta is a square. Part of one side is a zigzag.

New Brunswick is like a square—but not a very *square* square.

Saskatchewan has the straightest sides.

Manitoba has three straight sides and some lakes in the middle.

The biggest shape is the Northwest Territories.

British Columbia has islands along its west coast.

Some people have said that Ontario looks like a sleeping dragon. Can you find its ears and head?

23

40 Sometimes people use shortcuts to write the names of the provinces and territories. Look at the letters shown here. What do they stand for?

B.C.	Alta.	N.S.
Ont.	Que.	Nfld.
N.B.	N.W.T.	Man.
Y.T.	Sask.	P.E.I.

Where would they go on the map?

Answers to Bing Bongs, Quiz 1

12. Saskatchewan.
36. Manitoba.

2

Places
in Canada

1 Welcome back to *Turn On To Canada*. Our second quiz is called "Places in Canada." Canada is a *huge* country. There are kinds of places where *no one* lives. Name some of these places.

4 Cities are often far apart. What would you see in between the cities?

2 Most Canadians are found in places where a lot of people live fairly close together. What are these places called?

3 Most cities in Canada are near a United States border. Is this border in the north or south of Canada?

Purple violet
New Brunswick

30

5 We are going through the countryside. Name some things that you would *not* see in a city.

6 In the countryside there is lots of open space. In the city there is very little. As a city gets bigger there is less open space. People in the countryside live in rural communities. People in cities live in urban communities. Do you live in an urban or a rural community?

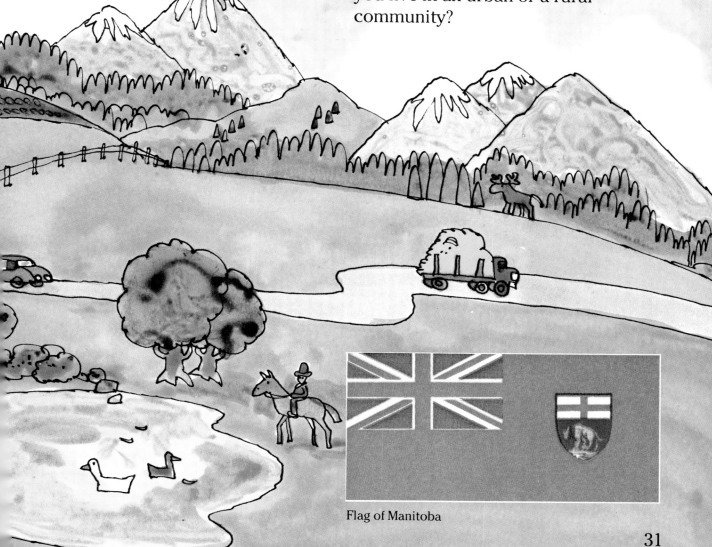

Flag of Manitoba

Prairie crocus
Manitoba

7 Here we are in a big city. How can you tell this is an urban community?

THEATRE

MAIN ST.

TH AVE.

JOSY'S CAFE

DANCE SCHOOL

JEWELLER LTD.

BOOKS

Joe's TRUCKING

BUS STOP

32

8 Name some things in this drawing that you would not see in the countryside.

9 Some people like the countryside. What would you like best about living in the country?

10 Other people like the city best. There are lots of different things to do. What are some exciting things about a city?

11 Which do you like best, the city or the country?

12 Cities can be different sizes. Put your right hand on this drawing so that your fingertips touch line 1. Cover up the rest of the drawing. See that little collection of houses and buildings? Many people would call this place a village.

13 Now pull your hand back to line 2. You could call this a town.

14 Pull back to line 3. What you see now is a small city.

15 If you draw your hand back to line 4, you'll see a larger city.

16 Finally take your hand away ... to find a huge city. Smaller places sometimes "grow together" to make up a big place. This large place is often called a metropolitan area.

Pacific dogwood
British Columbia

17
The biggest city in all of Canada is Toronto. More people live in the Toronto metropolitan area than in any other city in Canada. Can you find Toronto on the map?

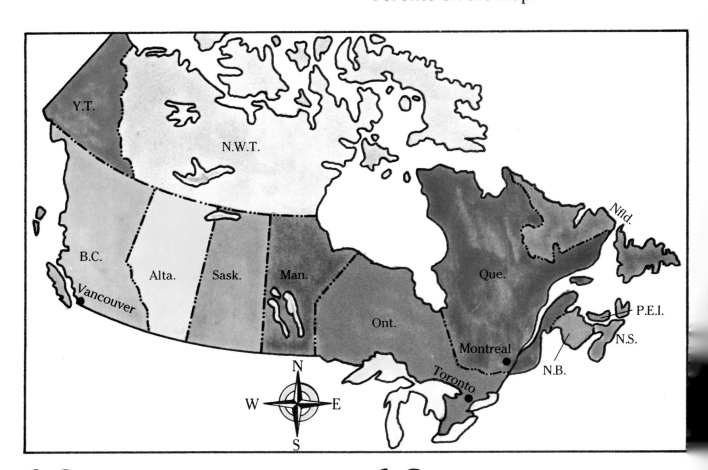

18
The next biggest city is the Montreal metropolitan area. Find it on the map.

19
Canada's third largest metropolitan area is in British Columbia. What is it?

22 Can you remember the special name of cities where the government makes the laws?

23 On the map on the next page, we have drawn stars for those special places. The black stars show the capitals of the provinces and territories. How many black stars are there?

24 Canada is one country, and it has a capital city, too. We have marked the capital of Canada with a blue star. What is the name of this special city?

25 Here's a Bing Bong! What kind of letter would you mail to a capital city?

Y.T.

Whitehorse ★

N.W.T.

★ Yellowknife

B.C.

Alta.

Edmonton
★

Sask.

Man.

Victoria ★

Regina
★

Winnipeg ★

Ont.

Que.

Quebec ★

Ottawa ☆

Toronto

26 What is the capital of British Columbia?

27 Which capital city is on one of the Great Lakes?

28 What else have you learned about that city?

29 Which capital city is farthest east?

30 The largest city in the province of Quebec is Montreal. Is Montreal also the capital city?

31 Name the capital cities which are on islands.

32 The prairie provinces are the three provinces between Ontario and British Columbia. What are their capitals?

33 The two capital cities farthest north are the capitals of territories. Name the territories and their capitals.

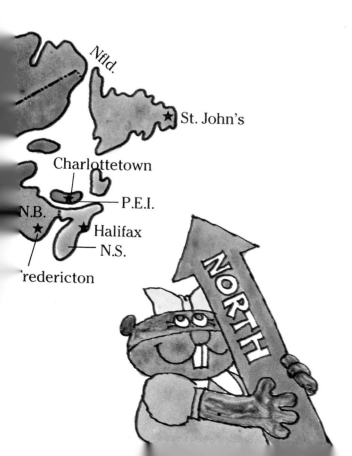

Nfld.

★ St. John's

Charlottetown

N.B.

P.E.I.

★ Halifax

N.S.

Fredericton

NORTH

34 Another Bing Bong!
Here comes Fred, the sign maker! He has letters for a sign showing the name of a capital city in eastern Canada.

Poor Fred!
What *is* that capital city?

35 Let's see how well you remember the provincial capitals. Put your fingers and thumbs on those dots and hold them there. Have someone call out the name of a province. Then you lift up the finger or thumb of the capital city of that province.

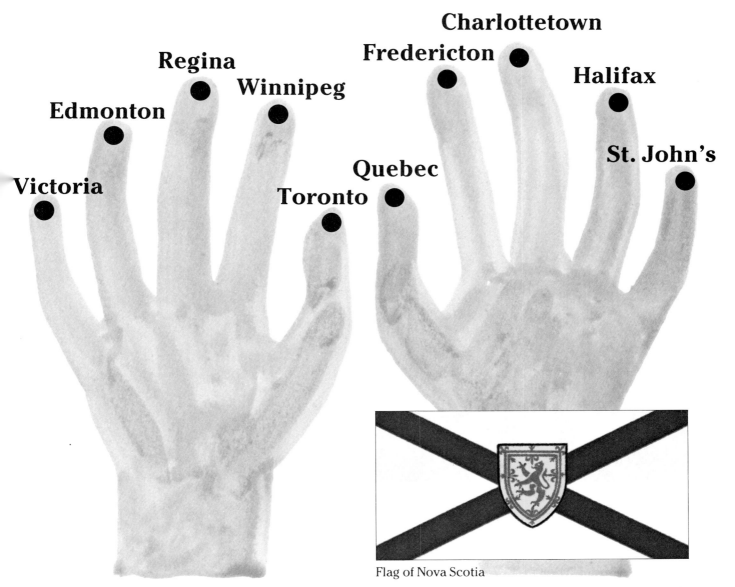

Flag of Nova Scotia

36 Remember that one city was shown with a blue star. Which city?

37 The government of Canada meets in Ottawa. It is also called the federal government. Ottawa is the most important capital city in Canada. Why?

38 Ottawa is the capital city for *all* of Canada. It is *your* capital city. What is your other capital city?

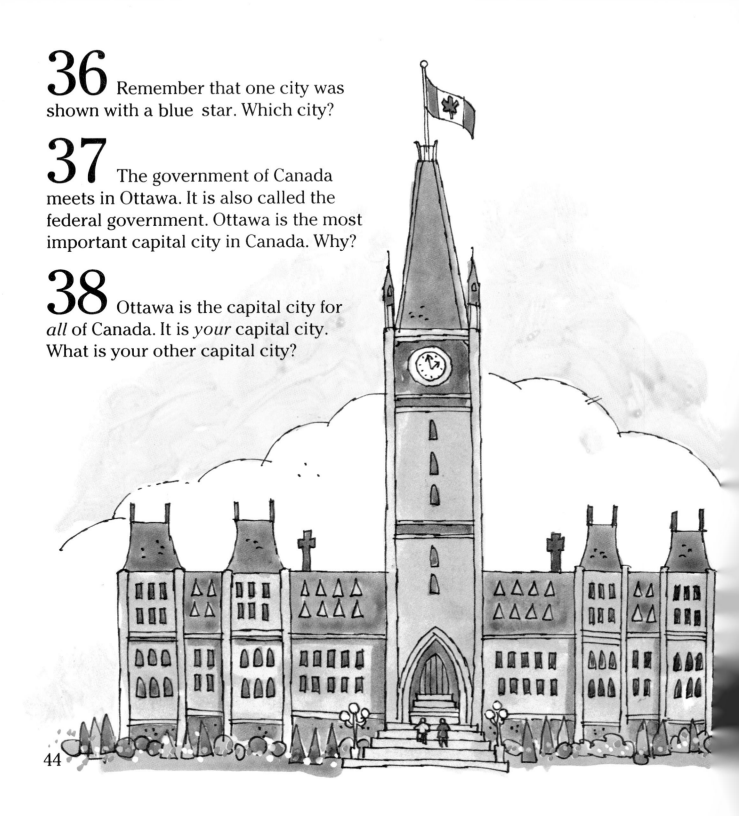

39 The flag on the Parliament Building in Ottawa is our country's flag. When you see this flag you think of Canada. What symbol is on the Canadian flag?

45

40 This game is
NEATO!

We have listed all the capital cities in Canada on this map. We have taken away the letters N, E, A, T and O.

Can you put them back in the correct way?

Whi_ _ _h_ rs_

_dm_ _ _

Vic_ _ri_

Y_ll_wk_if_

S_.J_h_'s

Ch_rl_ _ _ _ _ _w_

_gi_ _ _

Qu_b_c ★

H_lif_x

Wi_ _ip_g

Fr_d_ric_ _ _

N

W ——— E

S

_ _ _w_ ☆

_ _r_ _ _ _

47

3

Natural Resources of Canada

1 Welcome back to *Turn On To Canada*. Our third show is called "Natural Resources of Canada." Imagine that you are outside in the open air. You are sitting away up on top of a tree, looking around. You can see things far away. What things can you see that people have made?

50

r
w
has
tha

wa

6
and
do

ADANAC FISH CO

55

Pink lady's-slipper
Prince Edward Island

10 Most of our food grows on the land, not in the sea. Where would you see most farms?

a) mountains
b) flat land
c) rocky soil
d) on the ice in the far north

11 A lot of Canada's farmland is in Saskatchewan. There the land is flat. It is good for growing wheat. Name some foods that are made from wheat.

56

12 Prince Edward Island is called "the garden province." It is famous for a vegetable that can be eaten lots of ways. This vegetable can be mashed or boiled. It can be fried or baked. You probably like it cut very thin, fried and salted. What is this handy vegetable?

Flag of Saskatchewan

13 This map has a legend. It tells you what the picture symbols mean. Find the legend.

14 Apples are the most important fruit grown in Canada. Read the symbols to find where apples are grown.

15 Which provinces grow a lot of wheat?

16 Name two provinces that grow potatoes.

LEGEND

Wheat . . . .

Apples . . . .

Potatoes . . . .

NORTHWEST
TERRITORIES

NEWFOUNDLAND

MANITOBA

CHEWAN

QUEBEC

ONTARIO

PRINCE EDWARD
ISLAND

NOVA SCOTIA

NEW BRUNSWICK

N

W E

S

59

Prickly rose
Alberta

17 Some farms have animals. Name some animals that are kept for food.

18 Beef cattle are often kept in dry areas. Farms with beef cattle in Alberta and British Columbia are often very large. What is the special name for these large farms? (Hint: The word starts with "r" and has 5 letters.)

19 Butter and cheese are called dairy products. What are dairy products made from?

20 Which animal gives us these dairy products?

GRADE A

21 Name another dairy product.

22 It's Bing Bong time again!

What does a cow read to get the latest news?

23 Spaghetti means "little strings." You probably eat it with a sauce of tomatoes and beef. Maybe you sprinkle cheese on top. Some people add a fried egg. Can you trace all these foods back to a plant or animal?

24 There is one very large plant that we do not eat. Birds build nests in it. Boys and girls climb in it. People cut it down and build houses with it. What is this plant?

25 What happens to the trees after they are cut down?

26 What happens to the land after the forest is cut down?

27 The biggest trees in Canada grow in British Columbia. Why do they grow so large on the coast?

28 Canada makes more newsprint than any other country in the world. A lot of it comes from Quebec. What is newsprint used for?

29 Minerals are another natural resource. They are found in the ground. What are two ways miners get minerals out of the ground?

30 Have you ever heard pennies called "coppers"? Pennies and copper wire are made from the same mineral. What is the mineral?

31 Iron is used to make steel. Nickel helps to make steel stronger. Name some things made from steel.

32

Another Bing Bong!
Fill in one letter on each line.
You will find the missing mineral.

ACROSS
1. To cut, just a little
2. Rabbit
3. The missing mineral
4. To mail

DOWN
1. Not that
2. Not often
3. The missing mineral
4. To fix

	1	2	3	4
1	T	R		M
2	H	A		E
3				
4	S	E		D

33

There is a special mineral that is stringy. It is called asbestos. Quebec has a lot of asbestos. Asbestos does not burn, so you can make curtains and clothing that will not burn. There are certain people who need to wear clothing that does not burn. Who are they?

Flag of Quebec

34 Gasoline is a pinky white colour, but it is made from a thick black liquid. This liquid is pumped out of the ground. What is it called?

SWELL OIL

35 Most of Canada's oil comes from Alberta. Canadians are also looking for oil on the bottom of the Arctic Ocean and the Atlantic Ocean. Why would this be difficult?

36 Something else is often found in the ground with oil. You can't see it. You can't feel it. It's called natural gas. Why is it called *natural* gas?

37 People used to heat homes with another natural resource. Steam trains used it, too. They burned small chunks of a solid black mineral. What is it?

Madonna lily
Quebec

38 Natural gas and oil and coal are called energy resources. When they are burned, we can use the energy from them. And *another* kind of energy can be made from them. It makes lights and radios and TV sets go on. What is it called?

39 Electricity can also be made from the energy of rivers falling down a great height. Do you think a waterfall could make electricity?

40 Imagine that you went to a restaurant. You have some
   fish and chips
   a milkshake
   and apple pie with cheese for dessert.
Then you go to a store and buy a
   baseball bat
   and a copper bracelet.
You fill up the car with gasoline.
What natural resources have you used?

69

Answers to Bing Bongs, Quiz 3

22. The moos-paper.

32. The missing mineral is iron.

	1	2	3	4
1	T	R	I	M
2	H	A	R	E
3	I	R	O	N
4	S	E	N	D

4

Connections across Canada

1 This is the final show of *Turn On To Canada*. The producer calls it "Connections across Canada." We wanted to call it TELETELESHIPPOHIRADIAIRRASACO. The producer thought that word was too hard.

TELETELESHIPPOHIRADIAIRRASACO is really an easy way to remember all kinds of connections. Some of the letters stand for ways of talking to people in other places. That's called communication. Other letters tell ways of moving people and things. That's called transportation. You'll find out what the letters stand for.

Can you say this new word? Try this way:

telly
telly
SHIPPO
hi
RAIDY
air
ra
SACKO

TELE . . .

2 Your family probably has a wonderful little machine. You talk into it to speak to other people. What is this machine called?

3 What would you do if you *didn't* have a telephone and . . .
- a) you wanted to talk to a friend who lived far away?
- b) you wanted to call the fire department?

4 Time for a Bing Bong! What does a dog use to call another dog?

5 These people help you make telephone calls. Can you tell what they are doing?

TELEPHONE COMPANY

Flag of Prince Edward Island

75

TELETELE . . .

6 The telephone lets you have *two-way* communication. Someone talks to you. You can talk, too. Is television also two-way communication?

7 Do you think all commercials on TV are true? Why or why not?

8 Some TV shows are made in Canada. Many more come from the United States. Would you watch a Canadian or a U.S. program for:

   a) the weather?
   b) cartoons?
   c) the news?
   d) a football game in Toronto?
   e) a space launch?

TELETELESHIP . . .

9 The telephone and television are kinds of communication. Ships are a kind of transportation. They move people and things. In what parts of Canada would ships be most useful?

10 What do these ships carry?

11 Ships can load up with special boxes packed full of things. These boxes also fit onto trucks and trains. Why are these boxes a good idea?

TELETELESHIPPO . . .

12 If you send a letter to a friend, is that communication or transportation?

13 If you send a box of chocolates through the mail, is that communication or transportation?

14 Which is older, using the telephone or writing letters?

15 Does it cost more to telephone another city than to send a letter?

16 The Post Office asks you to use a postal code on your letters. How does the Post Office use this special code?

BING BONG

17 Here's a Bing Bong for you.

How many letters are there in THE LETTER CARRIER'S BAG?

Flag of New Brunswick

TELETELESHIPPOHIRADIAIR...

26 What is the *fastest* way to travel from city to city?

27 What is different about these planes?

28 What can carry more—a train or a plane?

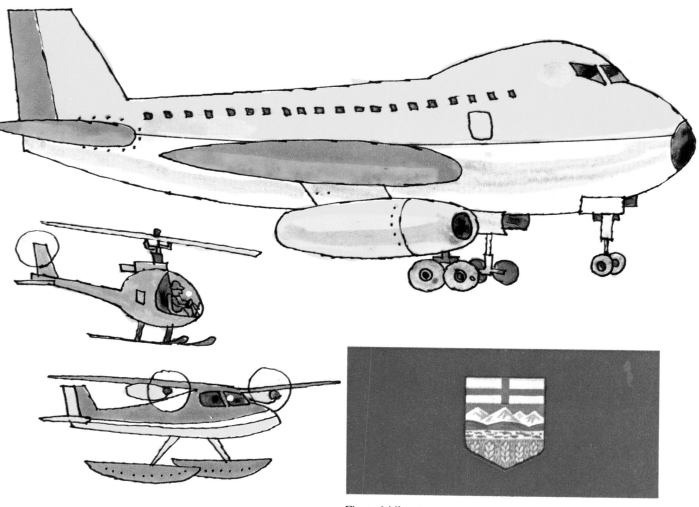

Flag of Alberta

TELETELESHIPPOHIRADIAIRRA . . .

29 There was a railway long before cars and planes went across Canada. About a hundred years ago, our country was joined from coast to coast by a railway. It was called the CPR. What do those letters stand for?

30 It was very difficult to build the railway through the Rocky Mountains. Why?

31 Not many people travel by train today. Can you think why?

32 Oh, oh, it's another Bing Bong. Why are the people on a good railway so polite?

33 These trucks are travelling "piggyback" on the train. Is this a good idea?

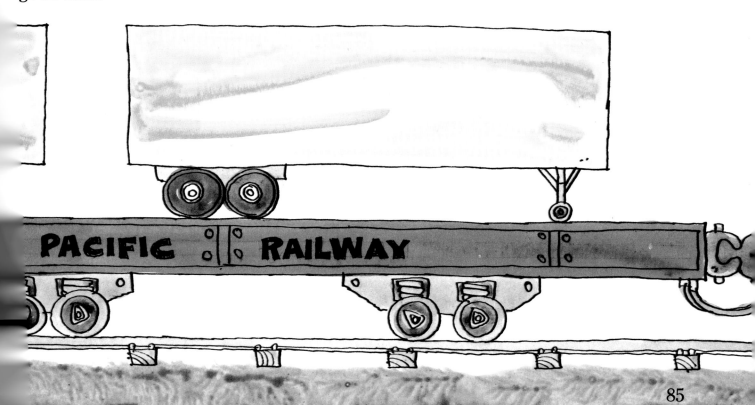

PACIFIC RAILWAY

TELETELESHIPPOHIRADIAIRRASA . . .

Mountain avens
Northwest Territories

86

34 Canada was the first country to use a satellite for long distance telephone calls. Where are satellites?

35 Satellites are also used for radio and TV shows. Signals are sent up to the satellite. Then they are bounced back to another place on Earth. Does this mean the signals can travel a long distance?

36 Satellites help you talk to other people when you are far apart. Why is a satellite a good idea for people in the Northwest Territories?

Flag of the Yukon Territory

87

TELETELESHIPPOHIRADIAIRRASACO!

Mayflower
Nova Scotia

37 This screen gives special information. What do you call this machine?

SUPER SAW

38 Computers help Canadians at work and at play. Computers can give you all kinds of information. What would *you* use a computer for?

39 Can you remember what the letters in
TELETELESHIPPOHIRADIAIRRASACO stand for?
Match the drawings to the right letters.

TELE
TELE
SHIP
PO
HI
RADI
AIR
RA
SA
CO

40 Here is something special which connects all Canadians. What is it?

O CANADA

O Canada! Our home and native land!
True patriot love in all thy sons command.
With glowing hearts we see thee rise,
The True North strong and free!
From far and wide, O Canada,
We stand on guard for thee.
God keep our land glorious and free!
O Canada, we stand on guard for thee.
O Canada, we stand on guard for thee.

O CANADA

O Canada! Terre de nos aïeux,
Ton front est ceint de fleurons glorieux!
Car ton bras sait porter l'épée,
Il sait porter la croix!
Ton histoire est une épopée
Des plus brillants exploits.
Et ta valeur, de foi trempée,
Protégera nos foyers et nos droits,
Protégera nos foyers et nos droits.

Answers to Bing Bongs, Quiz 4

4. A telebone.

17. Answer: 20 letters

the = 3
letter = 6
carrier's = 8
bag = 3
———
20

32. Because they are so well trained!

94

Acknowledgements

Photographs
NASA/Masterfile: p. 8; p. 9.
Alex Waterhouse-Hayward: pp. 4-5; p. 7;
p. 27; p. 49; p. 71; p. 95.
Illustrations
Jim Rimmer: all illustrations including the

covers, except for the following.
Ian Bateson: flag of Newfoundland; flowers
of provinces and territories.
Dennis Field: flags of provinces and
territories, except Newfoundland.
Reproduced from *Canada: Symbols of*

Sovereignty by Conrad Swan, York Herald
of Arms, by permission of University of
Toronto Press. © University of Toronto
Press, 1977.
Cartographic Consultant
Karen Ewing

Department of Education and Science

Safety in Outdoor Pursuits

DES Safety Series No 1

(Revised Spring 1977)

Other titles in this series:	*First published*
No. 2 Safety in Science Laboratories	**1973**
No. 3 Safety in Practical Departments	**1973**
No. 4 Safety in Physical Education	**1973**
No. 5 Safety in Further Education	**1976**
No. 6 Safety at School: General Advice	**1977**

London: Her Majesty's Stationery Office

ISBN 0 11 270378 X